STUDENT'S BOOK

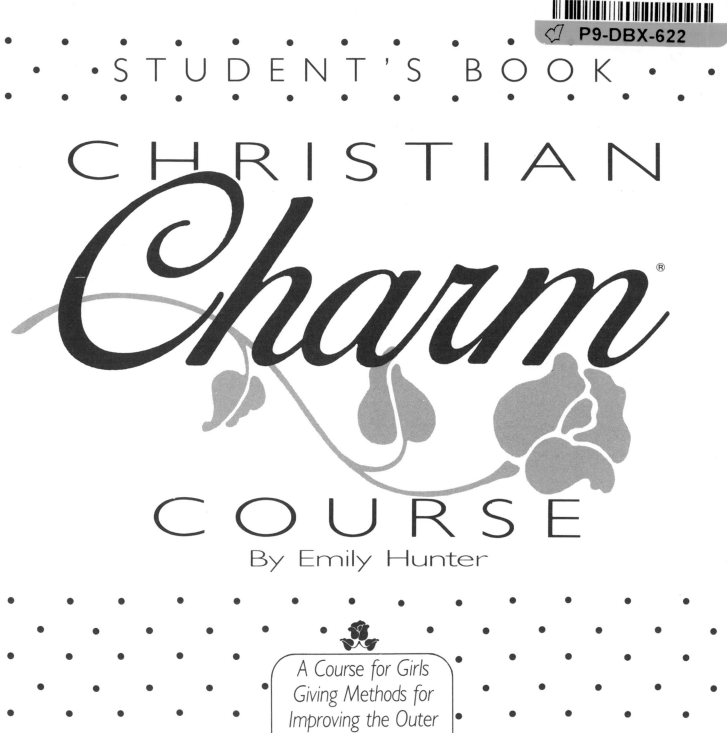

CHRISTIAN *Charm* COURSE

By Emily Hunter

A Course for Girls Giving Methods for Improving the Outer Appearance Along with Spiritual Instruction for Developing the True Beauty which Comes from a Heart surrendered to the Lord Jesus Christ

HARVEST HOUSE PUBLISHERS
Eugene, Oregon 97402

ACKNOWLEDGMENTS

Scripture quotations identified as WILLIAMS are reprinted by permission of Moody Press (The Moody Bible Institute of Chicago) from The New Testament, A Translation in the Language of the People by Charles B. Williams. Copyright © 1937, 1965.

CHRISTIAN CHARM COURSE—Student's Manual

Copyright © 1967, 1969, 1970, 1972, 1975, 1976, 1979, 1980 1981, 1984 by Wayne J. Hunter and Emily Hunter
Published by Harvest House Publishers
Eugene, Oregon 97402

ISBN-13: 978-0-89081-508-3
ISBN-10: 0-89081-508-9

Printed in the United States of America.

06 07 08 09 10 11 12 13 / ML / 45 44 43 42 41 40 39 38 37

❧ *A Word From Emily Hunter* ❧

Dear Pupil,

This is your personal notebook on Christian Charm. It will contain your personal measurements, your "before" and "after" pictures, fashion notes to flatter your particular figure, as well as many other practical reminders of the habits of charm you will be forming during this course.

May it also serve as a light for your feet, as you seek the path of true beauty—the inner beauty of love and holiness. For "Christian charm" encompasses not only the body, but also the spirit and soul. It is my prayer that this Christian Charm Course may serve as a guidepost pointing you to the One who can make your life truly joyful and beautiful forever—the Lord Jesus Christ.

Emily Hunter

The following personal development courses for group classes of Junior High and High School students utilize the "Teaching Bridge" approach which leads the students from practical instruction regarding their everyday interests to correlated spiritual instruction geared to meet the particular spiritual needs of their age group:

• FOR TEENAGE BOYS...

MAN IN DEMAND—Teacher's Book
MAN IN DEMAND—Student's Manual

• FOR TEENAGE GIRLS...

CHRISTIAN CHARM COURSE—Teacher's Book
CHRISTIAN CHARM COURSE—Student's Manual

These courses are ideally suited for use in Christian Day Schools, Youth Clubs, Family Night activities, Church Schools, Vacation Bible Schools, and Summer Bible Camps.

Available from your local Christian bookstore

HARVEST HOUSE™ PUBLISHERS
EUGENE, OREGON

Contents

CHRISTIAN Charm® COURSE

Posing Pointers

Posture

NO

YES

Body Profile

NO

YES

BEFORE THE CAMERA CLICKS,
CHECK THE FOLLOWING POINTS:

1.

2.

3.

4.

5.

6.

Facial Expression

NO

YES

Feet

NO

YES

Hands

NO

YES

Legs

NO

YES

A 'New Look' within and without

A "NEW LOOK" IN MY OUTWARD APPEARANCE

"For man looketh on the outward appearance, but the Lord looketh on the heart" (I Samuel 16:7).

"BEFORE"

Paste "Before"
Snapshot here.

(To be taken at beginning
of Christian Charm Course.)

"AFTER"

Paste "After"
Snapshot here.

(To be taken at completion
of Christian Charm Course.)

A "NEW LOOK" IN THE HEART AND LIFE

"Therefore if any man be in Christ, he is a new creature; old things are passed away; behold all things are become new" (II Corinthians 5:17).

"A new heart also will I give you, and a new spirit will I put within you: and I will take away the stony heart" (Ezekiel 36:26).

"BEFORE" THE NEW BIRTH

"The Bible can't be true! It doesn't make sense! Why should God call me a sinner when I'm doing the best I can? I've tried to make myself better, but I always fail! I don't see what difference it makes though! What I do with my life is nobody's business but my own! I can live the way I want and the more I get for myself the happier I'll be! But sometimes a queer hollow feeling creeps over me and I feel strangely dissatisfied. No matter how many new thrills I drum up, the excitement eventually wears off, and life seems empty again! I wish I knew what life's all about! I wonder if I could be missing out on something better! I guess I'm just one of those crazy mixed-up kids!"

"AFTER" THE NEW BIRTH

"It's just as if someone turned on the lights! Everything looks different. My attitudes have changed completely! Now I see things from God's point of view—not just my own selfish outlook. More than anything else I want to please the Lord! I thought this would be hard but I feel a strange new powerful strength within me helping me do right! Of course, I sometimes slip into sin, but immediately I ask the Lord to forgive me...and then I feel happy again! I have a real appetite for the Bible now—and, surprisingly, it makes beautiful sense! Most surprising of all is this overwhelming feeling of love in my heart! It begins with my love for the Lord, then overflows to everybody! At last I'm a real person!"

Taking a Look at Myself Spiritually

DO I NOW POSSESS SPIRITUAL LIFE?   (See I John 5:12.)

HAVE I BEEN GIVEN A NEW NATURE?   (See II Cor. 5:17.)

AM I A "BORN AGAIN" CHILD OF GOD?   (See John 1:12, 13.)

DO I HAVE EVERLASTING LIFE?   (See John 3:36.)

DOES MY FACE REFLECT THE IMAGE OF

CHRIST'S BEAUTY WITHIN ME?   (See II Cor. 3:18.)

HOW CAN I BECOME A CHRISTIAN?

I MUST REALIZE THAT I AM A SINNER.

"For all have sinned and come short of the glory of God" (Rom. 3:23).

I MUST RECOGNIZE THAT CHRIST PAID THE PENALTY FOR MY SIN.

"Christ died for our sins" (I Cor. 15:3).
"The wages of sin is death" (Rom. 6:23).

I MUST RECEIVE CHRIST, BELIEVING ON HIM AND TRUSTING HIM AS MY SAVIOUR.

"For God so loved the world, that He gave his only begotten son, that whosoever believeth in Him should not perish, but have everlasting life" (John 3:16). "The gift of God is eternal life through Jesus Christ" (Rom. 6:23).

CHRIST STANDS AT YOUR HEART'S DOOR . . .

If you have never received Christ into your life as Saviour, He stands now at the door of your heart waiting for you to invite Him in. "Behold, I stand at the door, and knock: if any man hear my voice and open the door, I will come in" (Rev. 3:20). The decision is yours. At this very moment you may ask Christ to come into your heart. Simply talk to Him in prayer, something like this:

PRAYER OF COMMITMENT:

Dear Jesus,
I humbly confess that I am a sinner.
I turn from my sin and come to you for forgiveness and mercy.
I believe you died on the cross to take my punishment for sin.
I receive you now as my own personal Saviour from sin.
I ask you to come into my heart just now.
Thank you for saving me and giving me everlasting life.
I want to follow you and obey you as Lord of my life.

The above prayer of commitment is an important step in the development of inner beauty. When a girl's heart has found peace with God, harsh tension lines relax; a new softness and gentleness appears; a lovely new radiance and glow--the light of His glory--shines through from within. Yes, a NEW LOOK WITHIN and a NEW LOOK WITHOUT go hand in hand. To be truly attractive, a girl must have both!

Looking Ahead...

I WANT A "NEW LOOK" IN MY OUTWARD APPEARANCE

I want to be attractive and charming, so that I will please others. I realize that this will not come about through wishful dreaming. I realize that I must work toward that goal diligently and steadfastly.

I WANT A "NEW LOOK" IN MY HEART AND LIFE

I want to be lovely and beautiful within, so that I will please God. I realize that I cannot change my heart merely by self-effort. I realize that I must allow God to enter my life and do His transforming work within me.

THEREFORE...

I will practice the rules of health and beauty presented during this Charm Course, insofar as I am able to do so.

☐ Yes, I will.

I will spend some time in God's presence each day. I will allow Him to talk to me through His Word and I will talk to Him in prayer, even though brief.

☐ Yes, I will.

A NEW LOOK "WITHOUT"

I would like to make the following improvements in my appearance:

1._____
2._____
3._____
4._____
5._____
6._____
7._____
8._____
9._____
10._____

A NEW LOOK "WITHIN"

I would like to see the following improvements made in the attitudes of my heart toward God, toward others, and toward myself:

1._____
2._____
3._____
4._____
5._____
6._____
7._____
8._____
9._____
10._____

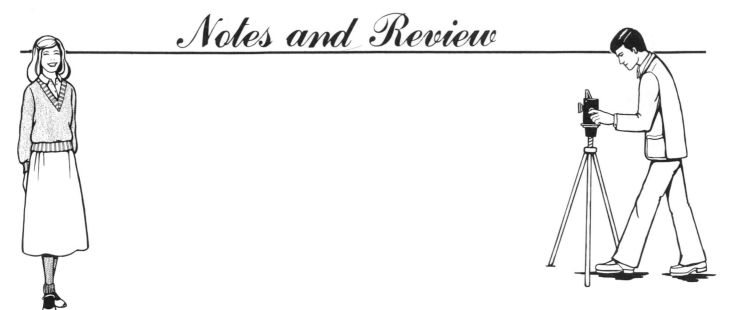

Notes and Review

1. *What are two basic reasons why a Christian girl should strive to look lovely?*

2. *Does a girl's attractiveness depend solely upon the characteristics she is born with?*

3. *Do you want to appear pleasing to the eyes of man? In Hebrews 4:13 we learn that our lives are* _____
   and _____ *to the eyes of God. Are you concerned with how you appear in the sight of God?*

4. *Would you like for others to see a photograph of your "soul"? Would you prefer that some "retouching" be done before it is placed on display?*

5. *What will bring a "new look" to the heart and life?*

6. *Will a "new look within" produce a "new look without" also? What happens?*

My Daily Diet

"Whether therefore ye eat, or drink, or whatsoever
ye do, do all to the glory of God" (I Cor. 10:31).

What did you eat in the last twenty-four hours? Did you choose the proper foods for smooth skin, sparkling eyes, shining hair, gleaming teeth, smooth nails, healthy nerves, vitality and pep? Compare your actual diet with the basic daily requirements. Score yourself as shown below.

MY ACTUAL DIET	BASIC DAILY REQUIREMENTS
BREAKFAST:	____ 4 glasses of milk (5 points each glass)
	____ one egg, 5 per week (10 points)
LUNCH:	____ whole grain cereal or bread (10 points)
	____ 3 pats of butter (10 points)
	____ one citrus fruit (10 points)
DINNER:	____ one other fruit (10 points)
	____ one poultry, fish, or meat (10 points)
	____ one green, leafy vegetable (10 points)
	____ one yellow vegetable (10 points)
SNACKS:	_____ TOTAL (Perfect score for beauty and health is 100 points.)

My Daily 'Half-Dozen'

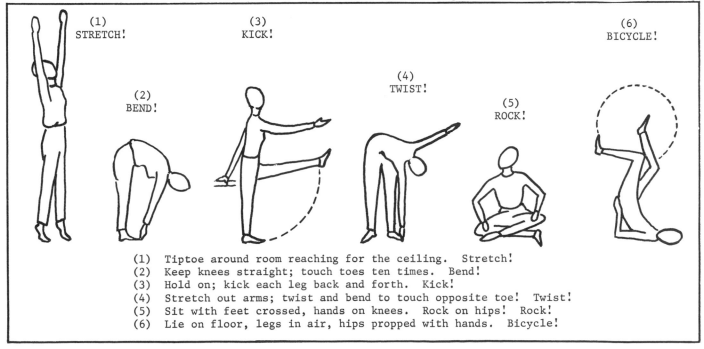

(1) STRETCH!
(2) BEND!
(3) KICK!
(4) TWIST!
(5) ROCK!
(6) BICYCLE!

(1) Tiptoe around room reaching for the ceiling. Stretch!
(2) Keep knees straight; touch toes ten times. Bend!
(3) Hold on; kick each leg back and forth. Kick!
(4) Stretch out arms; twist and bend to touch opposite toe! Twist!
(5) Sit with feet crossed, hands on knees. Rock on hips! Rock!
(6) Lie on floor, legs in air, hips propped with hands. Bicycle!

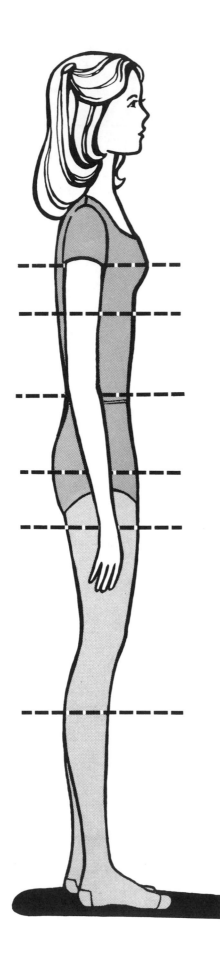

MEASURE AS FOLLOWS:

BUST - At largest dimension.

UPPER ARM - Halfway between elbow and shoulder.

WAIST - Level with elbow when arm is hanging down.

HIPS - At largest dimension.

THIGHS - At largest dimension.

CALF - At largest part.

NOTE:

Bust and hips should be equal, with waist ten inches smaller. A variation of two inches is allowable.

My Measurements

| | | | | 2|1 | | 2|2 | | 2|3 | | 2|4 | | 2|5 | | 2|6 | | 2|7 | | 2|8 | | 2|9 |

		WEIGHT	BUST	WAIST	HIPS	THIGH	CALF	UPPER ARM
Age _____	Start of Course							
Height _____	End of Course							

Measuring up Spiritually

AM I KEEPING SPIRITUALLY FIT?

"For bodily exercise profiteth little; but godliness is profitable unto all things, having promise of the life that now is, and of that which is to come" (I Timothy 4:8).

Do I show that I am spiritually alive by a healthy appetite for God's Word? ☐ Yes ☐ Somewhat ☐ No	"As newborn babes, desire the sincere milk of the word, that ye may grow thereby" (I Peter 2:2).
Am I well-nourished and strong? How often do I feed upon God's Word? ☐ Daily ☐ Occasionally ☐ Seldom	"Man shall not live by bread alone, but by every word that proceedeth out of the mouth of God" (Matthew 4:4).
Am I storing spiritual vitamins from the Holy Bible? Do I know more of God's Word today than a year ago? ☐ Yes ☐ Somewhat ☐ No	"Thy word have I hid in mine heart, that I might not sin against thee" (Psalm 119:11).
Do I stretch my spiritual muscles each morning by beginning my day with prayer, even if brief? ☐ Yes ☐ Occasionally ☐ Seldom	"In the morning will I direct my prayer unto thee, and will look up" (Psalm 5:3).
Do I practice relaxing exercises throughout the day by sending up thought prayers to God? ☐ Yes ☐ Occasionally ☐ Seldom	"Before they call, I will answer; and while they are yet speaking, I will hear" (Isaiah 65:24).
Do I preserve my spiritual stamina and vitality by casting off heavy burdens in prayer? ☐ Yes ☐ Occasionally ☐ Seldom	"Be careful for nothing; but in everything by prayer and supplication with thanksgiving let your requests be made known unto God" (Philippians 4:6).

"If a man does not exercise his arm he develops no biceps muscle; and if a man does not exercise his soul, he acquires no muscle in his soul, no strength of character, no vigor of moral fiber, nor beauty of spiritual growth." (Henry Drummond)

Calorie Chart

Angel food cake, medium piece..................	110
Apple pie, medium piece.......................	345
Apple, raw, medium............................	70
Applesauce, canned, 1/2 cup...................	115
Apricots with syrup, canned, 1/2 cup.........	110
Asparagus, cooked, 1/2 cup....................	18
Bacon, fried crisp, 1 strip..................	50
Banana, 1 medium..............................	85
Beans, snap, canned, 1/2 cup.................	23
Beef, pot-roast, lean and fat, 3 oz..........	245
Beef, pot-roast, lean only, 3 oz.............	168
Beef roast, lean and fat, 3 oz...............	165
Beef steak, broiled, lean only, 3 oz.........	172
Beets, cooked, diced, 1/2 cup................	25
Berry pie, medium piece.......................	340
Biscuit, 1 large..............................	140
Bologna, 1 medium slice.......................	86
Bread, white, 1 slice.........................	60
Bread, whole wheat, 1 slice...................	55
Broccoli, cooked, 1/2 cup.....................	20
Butter, 1 tablespoon..........................	100
Buttermilk, 1 cup.............................	90
Cabbage, cooked, 1/2 cup......................	17
Cake, plain, chocolate icing, medium piece...	370
Candy caramels, 1 oz..........................	115
Cantaloupe, 1/2 medium melon..................	30
Carbonated soft drinks, 8 oz..................	95
Carrots, cooked, 1/2 cup......................	22
Carrot, raw, (1)..............................	20
Cauliflower, cooked, 1/2 cup..................	13
Celery, raw, large stalk.....................	5
Cheese, American, 1-inch cube.................	70
Chicken, fried, 1 medium leg.................	90
Chicken, fried, 1/2 breast, 3 oz.............	172
Chicken noodle soup, canned, 1 cup...........	65
Chili con carne with beans, 1 cup...........	335
Clam chowder, canned, 1 cup..................	85
Cookie, plain, 1 large........................	120
Corn, canned, 1/2 cup.........................	85
Corn, cooked, 1 medium ear....................	70
Cornflakes, 1 oz..............................	110
Cottage cheese, 1/2 cup.......................	120
Cream, light, 2 tablespoons...................	60
Cream, whipped, 3 tablespoons................	83
Cupcake, plain without icing.................	145
Doughnut, cake, (1)..........................	125
Egg, boiled, 1 large..........................	80
Egg, scrambled with milk and fat, (1).......	110
Fig bar, 1 small..............................	55
Frankfurters, cooked, 1 medium...............	155
French fries, 10 pieces.......................	155
Fruit cocktail, canned, 1/2 cup.............	98
Fudge, plain, 1 oz............................	115
Gelatin dessert, plain, 1/2 cup.............	70
Graham crackers, 2 medium.....................	55
Grapefruit, raw, 1/2 medium..................	50
Grapenuts, 1/4 cup............................	110
Ham, lean, 3 oz...............................	245
Hamburger, broiled, 3 oz......................	245
Honey, 1 tablespoon...........................	65

Ice cream, 1/2 cup............................	148
Jelly or jam, 1 tablespoon...................	55
Lemon meringue pie, medium piece.............	305
Lettuce, 2 large leaves.......................	10
Macaroni and cheese, baked, 1/2 cup..........	235
Macaroni, cooked, 1/2 cup.....................	77
Margarine, 1 tablespoon.......................	100
Mayonnaise, 1 tablespoon......................	110
Milk, skim, 1 cup.............................	90
Milk, whole, 1 cup............................	160
Mince pie, medium piece.......................	365
Muffin, 1 medium..............................	140
Oatmeal, cooked, 1/2 cup......................	65
Orange, 1 medium..............................	60
Orange juice, fresh, 1 cup....................	115
Pancake, 1 medium.............................	60
Peach, fresh, 1 medium........................	35
Peaches with syrup, canned, 2 halves........	90
Peanut butter, 1 tablespoon..................	95
Pear, fresh, 1 medium.........................	100
Pears with syrup, canned, 2 halves..........	90
Peas, canned, 1/2 cup.........................	83
Pineapple with syrup, canned, 1 slice.......	90
Plum, fresh, 1 medium.........................	25
Plums with syrup, canned, 3 medium..........	100
Popcorn, ready-to-eat, 1 cup.................	65
Pork chop, 1 medium...........................	260
Potato, baked, 1 medium.......................	90
Potato, boiled, 1 medium......................	80
Potato chips, 10 large........................	110
Pumpkin pie, medium piece.....................	275
Raspberries, fresh, 1/2 cup..................	35
Rice, white, 1/2 cup..........................	92
Roll, plain, pan..............................	115
Salad dressing, French, 1 tablespoon........	60
Salmon, canned, 3 oz..........................	120
Sherbet, orange, 1/2 cup......................	130
Shredded wheat, 1 oz..........................	100
Soda cracker, (1).............................	25
Spaghetti with meat balls, 1 cup............	335
Spinach, cooked, 1/2 cup......................	22
Squash, summer, cooked, 1/2 cup.............	15
Squash, winter, baked, 1/2 cup...............	65
Strawberries, fresh, 1 cup...................	55
Sugar, granulated, 1 tablespoon.............	45
Tomatoes, canned, 1/2 cup.....................	25
Tomatoe, fresh, 1 medium......................	35
Tomatoe juice, canned, 1 cup.................	45
Tomatoe soup, canned, 1 cup..................	90
Tuna fish, drained, canned, 3 oz............	170
Veal roast, 3 oz..............................	230
Vegetable soup, canned, 1 cup................	80
Waffle, 1 average.............................	210
Watermelon, 1 average wedge..................	115
Wheat flakes, 1 oz............................	100

My Bible Reading Chart

New Testament Books	READ ONE CHAPTER PER DAY. CHECK OFF EACH CHAPTER WHEN FINISHED.																											
	1	2	3	4	5	6	7	8	9	10	11	12	13	14	15	16	17	18	19	20	21	22	23	24	25	26	27	28
Matthew																												
Mark																												
Luke																												
John																												
Acts																												
Romans																												
I Corinthians																												
II Corinthians																												
Galatians																												
Ephesians																												
Philippians																												
Colossians																												
I Thessalonians																												
II Thessalonians																												
I Timothy																												
II Timothy																												
Titus																												
Philemon																												
Hebrews																												
James																												
I Peter																												
II Peter																												
I John																												
II John																												
III John																												
Jude																												
Revelation																												

My Prayer List

PRAYER REQUESTS	AN-SWERED	PRAYER REQUESTS	AN-SWERED
1.		10.	
2.		11.	
3.		12.	
4.		13.	
5.		14.	
6.		15.	
7.		16.	
8.		17.	
9.		18.	

<u>N O T E :</u>

<u>TO MAKE USE OF THE PERSONAL BIBLE READING CHART</u>
<u>AND PRAYER LIST, REMOVE THIS PAGE FROM NOTEBOOK</u>
<u>AND PLACE IN YOUR BIBLE FOR EASY REFERENCE.</u>

(Cut along dotted line near center margin.) ⟶

Spiritual Food and Exercise

A "MUST" FOR GROWTH AND BEAUTY

"But grow in grace, and in the knowledge of our Lord and Saviour Jesus Christ" (II Peter 3:18).

TIPS TO HELP YOU

1. Select a Bible with easy-to-read print.

2. Dedicate a definite time each day for Bible study and prayer.

3. Choose the easier portions of the Bible to read first. Begin with the Gospels.

4. Before opening God's Word, open your heart to God. Ask Him to show you the truths He would have you learn.

5. Mark your Bible. If a verse holds special significance for you, underline it.

6. Pray aloud if possible. Even a whisper helps. "Mental" praying allows thoughts to wander.

7. Remember that you are always close to God's ear. In distress, breathe a quick S.O.S. prayer--in joy, a quick "thank you!"

8. Keep a prayer list. Make definite requests.
   "I need patience with _____."
   　　　　　　　　　　　(Name the person.)
   "I need victory over _____."
   　　　　　　　　　　　(Name the habit.)
   "I need faith to conquer_____."
   　　　　　　　　　　　(Name the fear.)

9. Base your requests upon God's promises in the Word. Make sure you fulfill the conditions to the promises.

10. Examine your requests: Are they according to God's will? Are you asking for anything forbidden in His Word?

11. Examine your motives: Are your requests for the glory of God or for selfish purposes?

12. When all is in order, pray with confidence. Expect answers. Though they may be delayed for God's own purposes, they will come. Do whatever God lays upon your heart as you wait.

CREATE IN ME THY BEAUTY NOW
(See music on inside back cover.)

Dear God, I come before you now
　　　To open up your Word.
My mind is full of scattered thoughts;
　　　My view of you is blurred.

Please help me read with open eyes
　　　Enlightened by Thy grace.
Help me to see on every page
　　　My lovely Saviour's face.

* * *

Dear God, your Word has searched my heart;
　　　It made me look within.
For when I saw my Saviour's face,
　　　I also saw my sin.

I saw the thorns upon His brow;
　　　I saw Him crucified.
And then I saw my careless life,
　　　My selfishness and pride.

* * *

Dear Lord, forgive...remold...renew
　　　As on Thy face I gaze.
Create in me Thy beauty now
　　　In tender girlhood days.

Remove the stains that smudge and blur,
　　　So all may clearly see
The image of your loveliness
　　　Reflected now in me!　　　--E.H.

Notes and Review

1. The average daily calorie requirement for a teenage girl is approximately _____ calories.

2. Extra pounds accumulate not only from over- _____, but also from under- _____.

3. The most beautiful girl is not always the one that others feel most drawn to.   Why is this?

4. How can spiritual neglect hinder the development of your personality?

5. How do daily devotions help to build a lovely personality?

6. No other personality is so attractive and magnetic as that of Jesus Christ.   What will happen to you as you draw close to Christ and spend time in His Presence?

Is My Posture Lovely?

HOW DO I HOLD MY HEAD?

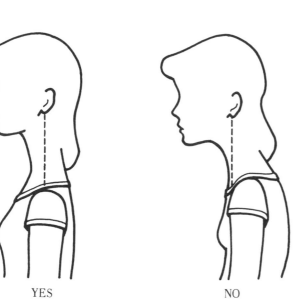

YES   NO

CAN I PASS THE PENCIL TEST?

Does the center of my ear-lobe line up vertically with the center of my shoulder-bone?

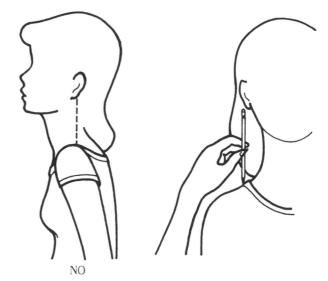

NO

HOW DO I STAND?

CAN I PASS THE PLUMB-LINE TEST?

Line should intersect center of ear-lobe, center of shoulder-bone, center of hip-bone, and less than one inch in front of ankle-bone.

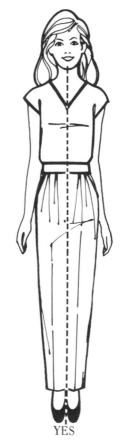

NO   NO   NO   YES   YES

Do I Walk and Sit Gracefully?

NO   NO   YES

TO WALK GRACEFULLY

DO . . .

Glide smoothly.
Hold head high.
Remain vertical from hips up.
Swing out from hips smoothly.
Keep stride moderate.
Point feet in a straight line.

DO NOT . . .

Swish knees noisily.
Drag or click heels.
Over-swing arms.
Over-reach stride.
Drop heels with a thud.
Slant head or chest forward.
Sway hips unnecessarily.

TO SIT DOWN SMOOTHLY

DO . . .

Touch knees to back of chair.
Lower yourself, keeping erect.
Sit down. Slide back into place.

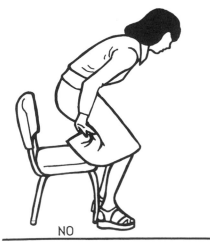

DO NOT . . .

Reach backward with
    buttocks.
Slide palms tightly
    across hips to
    smooth skirt.
Wriggle back into
    chair with
    snake hips.
Give full skirts a
    forward fling,
    flopping hem
    high in air.

NO

TO ASSUME A PRETTY SITTING POSTURE

DO . . .

Keep knees together, ankles together.
Sit tall with hands in lap.
Cross legs above knees, holding legs
    close together.

DO NOT . . .

Sprawl like a floppy
    rag doll.
Recline in chair, slid-
    ing hips forward.
Twist feet around chair
    legs.
Cross your arms.
Draw legs under
    chair.

NO

My Daily Christian Walk

"Walk in the Spirit, and ye shall not fulfill the lust of the flesh" (Galatians 5:16).

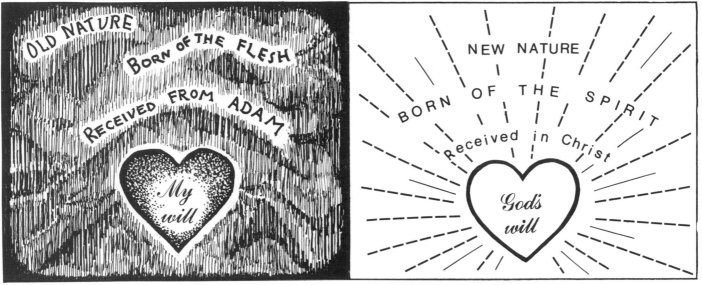

(Choose proper "spiritual antidote" from right column; place number in box at left.)

MY ATTITUDE OF HEART "WALKING AFTER THE FLESH"	MY ATTITUDE OF HEART "WALKING IN THE SPIRIT"
1 ☐ "One more time...and I'll BLOW MY TOP!"	(1) "Let me not forget I am not my own. I am bought with a price! May I thus live to please you, Lord!" (I Cor. 6:19,20)
2 ☐ "But I've seen other Christians doing it...so WHY CAN'T I?"	(2) "May I forgive others, Lord, even as you have forgiven me!" (Eph. 4:32; Matt. 5:44)
3 ☐ "I just CAN'T break that habit! There is no use trying!"	(3) "Not my human wisdom, Lord, but your divine wisdom!" (Jas. 1:5; I Cor. 3:19)
4 ☐ "Of course, I know what's best for me! Do you think I'm STUPID?"	(4) "May I not grieve Thy Holy Spirit in the slightest way today--not once!" (Eph. 4:30; Eccl. 12:14)
5 ☐ "But Mom...ALL the girls are wearing them!"	(5) "Give me Thy patience just now!" (James 1:3,4; Rom. 5:3)
6 ☐ "Just this once won't hurt! No one will know!"	(6) "May I glorify you, Jesus, in everything--yes, even in my dress!" (I Tim. 2:9; I Cor. 10:31)
7 ☐ "Mom's OLD-FASHIONED! Times have changed! I'll stay out as late as I please!"	(7) "Others might lead me astray! Help me to keep my eyes fixed on you, Lord!" (Heb. 12:2)
8 ☐ "It's MY life! I'll live it any way I please!"	(8) "Lord, I am weak! Give me your strength to overcome this sin in my life!" (I Cor. 10:13)
9 ☐ "She treated me horribly! I'll never forgive her! I'll get even if it's the last thing I do!"	(9) "Even when I can't understand their reasons, Lord, help me obey my parents to honor your command!" (Eph. 6:1,2)

Reverse sheet to read answers: ·(2)-6 ;(1)-8 ;(9)-7 ;(4)-6 ;(6)-5 ;(3)-4 ;(8)-3 ;(7)-2 ;(5)-1

As I Walk Through Life

I must remember that...

A lovely posture and a graceful carriage are essential to charm. But I will never appear charming to others if I do not also cultivate a beautiful spiritual posture and a pleasing Christian walk in my day-to-day life!

A GIRL WILL NEVER BE CHARMING--no matter how light her step--if she walks roughshod over others!

A GIRL WILL NEVER BE CHARMING--no matter how regal her bearing--if she holds her head high in arrogance and self-conceit!

A GIRL WILL NEVER BE CHARMING--no matter how carefully she places her feet one before the other in a straight line--if she cannot walk a straight line with others, if she is crooked in her dealings, deceitful, disloyal, untrue!

A GIRL WILL NEVER BE CHARMING--no matter how graceful her body motions--if she walks awkwardly with her friends, shoving them thoughtlessly aside to suit her selfish whims!

A GIRL WILL NEVER BE CHARMING--no matter how gently she places her heels on the floor--if she "kicks others around" in her eagerness to get to the top!

A GIRL WILL NEVER BE CHARMING--no matter how harmoniously her muscles are coordinated--if she is out of harmony with her Creator, out of harmony with family and friends, demanding her way above theirs.

God wants me...

To walk after His commandments	II John 6
To walk worthy of the Lord	Colossians 1:10
To walk honestly	I Thessalonians 4:12
To walk wisely	Proverbs 28:26
To walk humbly	Micah 6:8
To walk circumspectly	Ephesians 5:15
To walk uprightly	Proverbs 10:9
To walk by faith	II Corinthians 5:7
To walk in truth	III John 4
To walk in the Spirit	Galatians 5:16
To walk in the fear of the Lord	Acts 9:31
To walk in the steps of Jesus	I Peter 2:21

Notes and Review

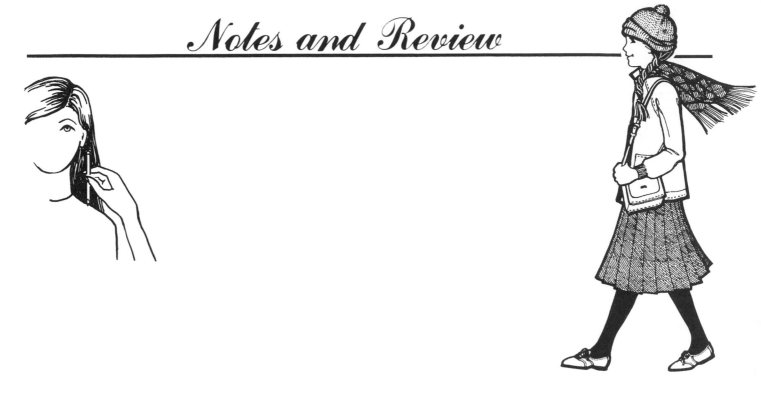

1. How I carry my _____ determines to a large degree my total posture.

2. When I allow my head to sag or droop, my shoulders _____, my chest _____ and my waistline _____ .

3. For proper posture, my buttocks should be pushed _____ and _____ , and my tummy should be pulled _____ and _____ .

4. What will determine my "spiritual posture" when I stand before God? What will enable me to stand before Him in confidence unashamed (I John 2:28)?

5. What does God promise those who walk in His ways (Psalm 128:1, 2)?

Facial 'Beauty From Without'

(Fill in the blank spaces with the proper words.)

①

To rate a clear complexion
That's lovely as a dream,
Be ultra-conscientious
In the way you cleanse and cream.

FOR COMPLEXION BEAUTY . . . .

Use_____and_____strokes

    in all creaming and cleansing.

If skin is oily, cleanse with_____.

Use_____for dry skin

    and remove with_____.

②

Don't panic over pimples!
Don't shed a single tear!
Just follow these instructions,
And watch them disappear!

WHEN YOUR FACE BREAKS OUT . . .

Avoid_____foods.

Keep your_____off your face.

Wash your face at least_____times daily.

Wash your_____frequently.

Consult a_____for advice.

③

When going to a masquerade,
We paint a gawdy face,
But "natural" makeup is the rule
For every other place!

FOR A LOVELY, NATURAL APPEARANCE . . .

Choose_____shades of lipstick.

Avoid too _____ or too

_____ a shade of liquid base.

Remember that it's difficult to use_____

_____and still look "natural."

④

Some things about our faces
Make us pout and sulk and fret.
But this just calls attention
To the things we should forget!

FORGET THESE--AND OTHERS WILL TOO . . .

Your_____
    (Wear them confidently!)

Your_____
    (Never cover them with your hands!)

Your_____
    (They give a sunny, wholesome appearance!)

Facial 'Beauty From Within'

WHAT DOES YOUR FACE REVEAL?
Take a check-list of your heart:

Kindness	☐
Contentment	☐
Love	☐
Gentleness	☐
Patience	☐
Friendliness	☐
Cheerfulness	☐
Optimism	☐
Humility	☐
Peace	☐

Unkindness	☐
Discontent	☐
Hatred	☐
Harshness	☐
Impatience	☐
Unfriendliness	☐
Dejection	☐
Pessimism	☐
Haughtiness	☐
Guilt	☐

WHO'S THE FAIREST?

Mirror, mirror on the wall...
  Who's the fairest of them all?
Not the girl with hateful heart,
  Poison tongue like stinging dart.
Fairest she, who sheds forth love,
  Gentle thoughts from God above.
Beauty blossoms in the face
  When the heart is filled with grace.

Mirror, mirror on the wall...
  Who's the fairest of them all?
Not the girl with sullen eye,
  Pouting lips that fret, defy.
Fairest she, whose moods are bright,
  Happy rainbows of delight.
Faces wreathed in joy declare
  God's own beauty dwelling there.

Mirror, mirror on the wall...
  Who's the fairest of them all?
Not the unchaste, brazen maid,
  Flaunting, flippant, unafraid.
Fairest she, whose heart is pure,
  Manner modest, glance demure.
Virtue crowns this girl a queen
  For her life shines true and clean.

Mirror, mirror, tell me who
  Can my countenance renew?
Jesus Christ, God's righteous Son,
  Altogether Lovely One!
Fairest of Ten Thousand! Yes,
  He can give you loveliness!

--E.H.

"For as he thinketh in his heart, so is he." Proverbs 23:7

"A merry heart maketh a cheerful countenance" (Proverbs 15:13).

"Let the beauty of the LORD our God be upon us" (Psalm 90:17).

"The beauty of holiness..." (Psalm 96:9)..."The ornament of a meek and quiet spirit" (I Peter 3:4).

She was as good as she was fair.
None, none on earth above her!
Pure in thought as angels are:
To know her was to love her.
(Samuel Rogers)

"Though thou clothest thyself with crimson, though thou deckest thee with ornaments of gold, though thou rentest thy face with painting, in vain shalt thou make thyself fair" (Jeremiah 4:30).

"The shew of their countenance doth witness against them; and they declare their sin...they hide it not" (Isaiah 3:9).

The false, the deceit that you bear in your heart;
Will not stay inside where it first got a start;
For sinew and blood are a thin veil of lace...
What you wear in YOUR HEART, you wear in YOUR FACE!
(Author unknown)

Notes and Review

1. *What is the difference between "facial beauty" and "facial appeal"?*

2. *To insure a lovely "facial posture," I should not* _____ *my eyebrows,* _____ *my lips,* _____ *my eyes,* _____ *my teeth, or* _____ *my jaws.*

3. *For a radiant smile, I should: (mark true or false)*

   _____ *Extend my lipstick beyond my natural lip margins.* _____ *Show my teeth.* _____ *Hold my lips tight together.* _____ *Close my eyes as I smile.* _____ *Remove lipstick smudges from my teeth.* _____ *Cover my teeth braces with my hands.*

4. *How does a girl's attitude toward herself affect her countenance?*

5. *Can a girl be truly pretty if her heart is "ugly?"*

6. *Can God transform a girl's facial appearance?*

Rules for Healthy Shining Hair

BRUSH HAIR DAILY . . .

1. to sweep away dirt and dust
2. to stimulate the scalp
3. to add luster and sheen

NOT LIKE THIS...BUT THIS!

NOT DOWN.....UP AND OUT!

KEEP HAIR TOOLS CLEAN!

Remove loose hair and lint from brush each day. Wash out rollers, clips, barrettes, comb and brush each time you wash your hair. Dry brush with bristles downward. Curling iron and electric rollers may be wiped with a damp cloth.

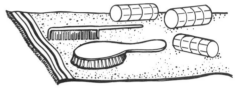

GIVE THEM A SUDSY BATH!

THEN LAY ON TOWEL TO DRY

SHAMPOO ON SCHEDULE!

Determine perfect schedule; then follow carefully. Wash hair as soon as mirror reveals telltale symptoms that rob hair of beauty. Shampoo regularly to keep hair clean...fragrant...sparkling... healthy...vibrant...beautiful!

WHEN HAIR BEAUTY DISAPPEARS...

IT'S TIME TO SHAMPOO AGAIN!

RINSE...RINSE... AND RINSE AGAIN!

Use "oceans of water!" A spray hose helps. Follow with vinegar rinse to remove dulling soap film (1/2 c. to 1 qt. water). Rinse away aroma. Lemon rinse not only removes film but lightens hair also. Use cream rinse for softness and manageability on hard-to-control, tangly hair or on coarse, dry wiry hair.

SPRAY HOSE RINSES CRYSTAL-CLEAN

VINEGAR RINSE REMOVES SOAP FILM

MY PERSONAL HAIR CARE CHART

(To help form good habits of hair care, check items below for a period of 30 days.)

	1	2	3	4	5	6	7	8	9	10	11	12	13	14	15	16	17	18	19	20	21	22	23	24	25	26	27	28	29	30
Brushed hair																														
Washed out "hair tools"																														
Shampooed my hair today																														
Followed with rinse																														

As a Christian Girl, what should be

My Attitude Toward My Hair?

(Indicate which attitudes you consider "right" or "wrong" by checking appropriate blanks.)

I.   SHOULD I BE OVERLY CONCERNED WITH MY HAIR?

(a) I should spend every spare moment in front of the mirror so that I'll look as pretty as possible!   ☐ Right   ☐ Wrong

(b) I should pay little attention to my hair to avoid worldliness.   ☐ Right   ☐ Wrong

(c) I should take time to keep my hair clean, well-groomed and attractive.   ☐ Right   ☐ Wrong

"If a woman have long hair, it is a glory to her" (1 Corinthians 11:15).

II.   WHAT SHOULD BE MY MOTIVE IN STRIVING FOR LOVELY HAIR?

(a) To outdo the other girls in my class.   ☐ Right   ☐ Wrong

(b) To attract attention to myself.   ☐ Right   ☐ Wrong

(c) To be respected and admired so that my influence will count for Christ.   ☐ Right   ☐ Wrong

"Whatsoever ye do, do all to the glory of God" (1 Corinthians 10:31).

III.   SHOULD I CHOOSE AN EXTREME OR ELABORATE HAIRDO?

(a) A fancy and extreme hairdo will focus greater attention on me, and the more people that notice me the better!   ☐ Right   ☐ Wrong

(b) My hair style should be attractive, but always in keeping with modesty, simplicity and good taste.   ☐ Right   ☐ Wrong

"Let your moderation be known unto all men" (Philippians 4:5).

IV.   SHOULD I CHANGE THE BASIC COLOR OF MY HAIR?

(a) A new hair color will bring me the admiration I desire.   ☐ Right   ☐ Wrong

(b) I would gain nothing, but I would lose my unaffected naturalness.   ☐ Right   ☐ Wrong

(c) A false hair color would make me appear unsure of my personal worth.   ☐ Right   ☐ Wrong

"Whatsoever things are true...honest...just...pure...lovely..." (Philippians 4:8).

Notes and Review

1. Why should the time period between shampoos vary from one girl to another?

2. How can I determine the shampoo schedule that is correct for my hair?   What telltale signs should I watch for?

3. Why should a good brushing precede my shampoo?   Should a good brushing also follow my shampoo, as soon as my hair is dry?

4. After washing out my hairbrush, I should lay it on a towel to dry with bristles ☐ upward.   ☐ downward.

5. If my hair is thin and fine, my brush should have _____ bristles.

6. If my hair is thick and coarse, my brush should have _____ bristles.

7. How can I combat dandruff?

Creating 'Oval Beauty' With My Hair

THE MOST FLATTERING HAIR STYLE MAKES THE FACIAL CONTOUR APPEAR TO BE OVAL IN SHAPE.

IF MY FACE IS ROUND . . .

Not This ____

Do not wear hair flat on top or full at sides. Do not add to cheek width by covering your ears with bulky hair.

NO   YES

But This !

Add height with upward lift on top. Keep hair close to sides and smooth over ears (or expose ears.) Diagonal part with side dip or bang is good. Short, upswept hair is also becoming.

IF MY FACE IS PEAR-SHAPED . . .

Not This ____

Do not wear hair flat and smooth at temple. Avoid fullness at jaw line. Never fully expose your narrow forehead. Avoid focusing eye interest on lower portion.

NO   YES

But This !

Wear full wide bangs. Strive for fullness above ears and above temples. Keep eye interest in the upper portion. Always keep hair away from jaw line. (Long hair may fall flat and smooth over cheek, or gather it together at back of head.)

IF MY FACE IS HEART-SHAPED . . .

Not This ____

Do not expose your broad fore-head fully. Try to avoid fullness at the temple.

NO   YES

But This !

Always add fullness beneath your ears. Wear a side bang or dip, if possible. A diagonal part is also good.

IF MY FACE IS SQUARE . . .

Not This ____

Never wear hair flat on top or full at sides. Do not add full-ness at jaw line. Full, broad bangs are not good. Avoid straight, sharp lines.

NO   YES

But This !

Strive for upward lift on top. Keep hair close to sides and away from jaw line. Soft curves are good. So is diagonal part with side bang or dip. Either keep ears exposed or wear hair flat and smooth over them.

IF MY FACE IS LONG AND NARROW . . .

Not This ____

Never pile hair high on top. Do not draw hair away from forehead. Avoid straight, long hair.

NO   YES

But This !

Wear hair full at sides (covering ears). Keep your hair smooth and flat on top. A low side part with soft parted bangs is becoming. (Long hair should be worn with fluffiness or waves at side.)

Creating a Pretty Profile With My Hair

▶ Two different hair styles are shown for each facial profile and body type. Can you select the one that gives the most pleasing proportion and balance? Indicate your choice by placing YES or NO in the boxes below.

(Faces in each pair are identical)

LONG NECK

SHORT NECK

TALL

LARGE

PETITE

PROTRUDING CHIN AND FOREHEAD

RECEDING CHIN AND FOREHEAD

HIGH FOREHEAD

LOW FOREHEAD

SMALL FLAT NOSE

PROMINENT PROTRUDING NOSE

Styling Techniques

ROLLERS

- FOR WAVY FULLNESS
- FOR SOFT END CURL
- FOR BODY AND FULLNESS

REGULAR ROLLERS   ELECTRIC ROLLERS   HOME PERMANENT ROLLERS

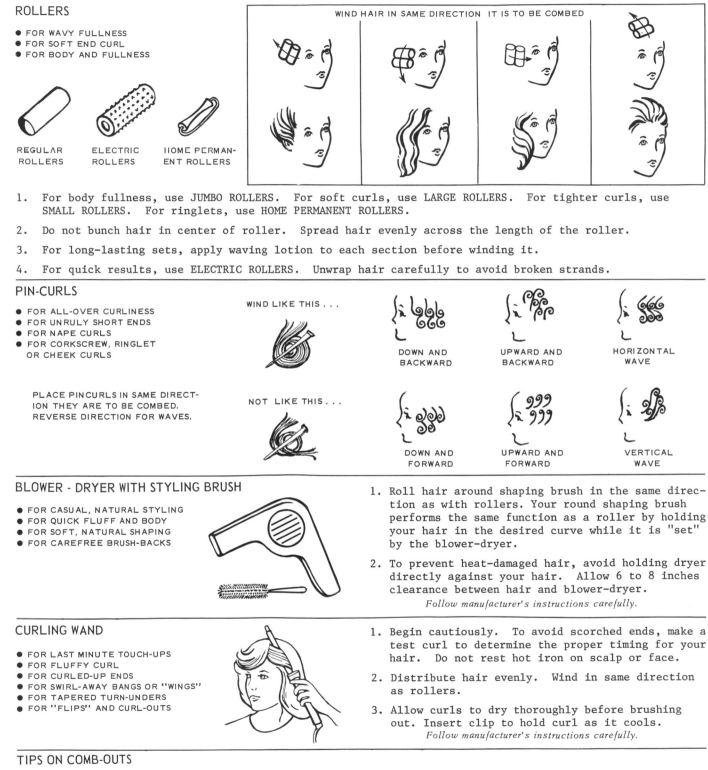

WIND HAIR IN SAME DIRECTION IT IS TO BE COMBED

1. For body fullness, use JUMBO ROLLERS. For soft curls, use LARGE ROLLERS. For tighter curls, use SMALL ROLLERS. For ringlets, use HOME PERMANENT ROLLERS.

2. Do not bunch hair in center of roller. Spread hair evenly across the length of the roller.

3. For long-lasting sets, apply waving lotion to each section before winding it.

4. For quick results, use ELECTRIC ROLLERS. Unwrap hair carefully to avoid broken strands.

PIN-CURLS

- FOR ALL-OVER CURLINESS
- FOR UNRULY SHORT ENDS
- FOR NAPE CURLS
- FOR CORKSCREW, RINGLET OR CHEEK CURLS

PLACE PINCURLS IN SAME DIRECTION THEY ARE TO BE COMBED. REVERSE DIRECTION FOR WAVES.

WIND LIKE THIS . . .

NOT LIKE THIS . . .

DOWN AND BACKWARD   UPWARD AND BACKWARD   HORIZONTAL WAVE

DOWN AND FORWARD   UPWARD AND FORWARD   VERTICAL WAVE

BLOWER - DRYER WITH STYLING BRUSH

- FOR CASUAL, NATURAL STYLING
- FOR QUICK FLUFF AND BODY
- FOR SOFT, NATURAL SHAPING
- FOR CAREFREE BRUSH-BACKS

1. Roll hair around shaping brush in the same direction as with rollers. Your round shaping brush performs the same function as a roller by holding your hair in the desired curve while it is "set" by the blower-dryer.

2. To prevent heat-damaged hair, avoid holding dryer directly against your hair. Allow 6 to 8 inches clearance between hair and blower-dryer.
    Follow manufacturer's instructions carefully.

CURLING WAND

- FOR LAST MINUTE TOUCH-UPS
- FOR FLUFFY CURL
- FOR CURLED-UP ENDS
- FOR SWIRL-AWAY BANGS OR "WINGS"
- FOR TAPERED TURN-UNDERS
- FOR "FLIPS" AND CURL-OUTS

1. Begin cautiously. To avoid scorched ends, make a test curl to determine the proper timing for your hair. Do not rest hot iron on scalp or face.

2. Distribute hair evenly. Wind in same direction as rollers.

3. Allow curls to dry thoroughly before brushing out. Insert clip to hold curl as it cools.
    Follow manufacturer's instructions carefully.

TIPS ON COMB-OUTS

1. For a lasting set, refrain from brushing out hair until it is thoroughly dry.

2. After removing rollers, etc., give hair a good brushing to break up any curl separation.

3. For curl-under: Insert hand UNDER hair. Brush smoothly DOWN AND UNDER edge of hand, cupping ends.

4. For curl-out: Place hand on TOP of hair. Brush ends UP AND OVER edge of hand.

5. For fluffy ends: Twirl brush UP and OUT at end of each stroke.

Femininity—My 'Crowning Glory'

"Whose adorning let it not be that outward adorning of plaiting the hair...but let it be the hidden man of the heart" (I Peter 3:3,4). "The King's daughter is all glorious within" (Psalm 45:13).

HONOR
PURITY
SELF-CONTROL
A CLEAN HEART
VIRTUE
SWEETNESS
A DEMURE MANNER
A QUIET SPIRIT
CHASTITY
MODESTY

TO BE TRULY FEMININE . . .

▶ SEE THAT YOU LOOK LIKE A GIRL --NOT A BOY

"But if a woman have long hair it is a glory to her" (I Corinthians 11:15).

"The woman shall not wear that which pertaineth unto a man, neither shall a man put on a woman's garment" (Deuteronomy 22:5).

▶ DON'T USURP THE ROLE OF THE MALE

"But I suffer not a woman...to usurp authority over the man...for Adam was first formed, then Eve" (I Timothy 2:12,13).

"The weaker vessel" (I Peter 3:7). "An help meet for him" (Genesis 2:18).

▶ CULTIVATE A QUIET, GENTLE SPIRIT

"The ornament of a meek and quiet spirit, which is in the sight of God of great price" (I Peter 3:4).

"Gentle, showing all meekness unto all men" (Titus 3:2).

▶ VALUE YOUR CHASTITY

"Who can find a virtuous woman? for her price is far above rubies" (Proverbs 31:10).

"Your body is the temple of the Holy Ghost which is in you" (I Corinthians 6:19).

"Keep thyself pure" (I Timothy 5:22).

How Feminine am I?

Do my "feminine" qualities outnumber my "unfeminine" qualities? (Check list below.)

THESE DESTROY FEMININITY - THESE INCREASE FEMININITY

☐ A bulky, flabby figure....A trim, disciplined body ☐
☐ Sluggishness.............................Vitality ☐
☐ An unkempt appearance............Careful grooming ☐
☐ Mannish attire...........Dainty, pretty clothing ☐
☐ Older, daring styles......Youthful, girlish styles ☐
☐ Revealing clothes...............Modesty in dress ☐
☐ Over-display in dress....Quiet, conservative dress ☐
☐ Gawdy makeup......................"Natural" makeup ☐
☐ Mannish, short hairdos...........Soft, clean hair ☐
☐ A dead-pan face.....................A ready smile ☐
☐ Tobacco odors................A delicate fragrance ☐
☐ Stained fingers...............Clean, lovely hands ☐
☐ Smoking cigarettes........Abstaining from tobacco ☐
☐ Drinking liquor............Abstaining from liquor ☐
☐ Telling off-color jokes..............Clean speech ☐
☐ Reading smutty books.......Purity of thought life ☐
☐ An ungainly walk..........A lovely, graceful walk ☐
☐ Sprawling in chairs.............Sitting prettily ☐
☐ A slouching posture..........A queen-like posture ☐
☐ A "loud" mouth.................Soft, gentle speech ☐
☐ Raspy, gravelly voice........Pleasant vocal tones ☐
☐ Slangy expressions...........A refined vocabulary ☐
☐ Malicious gossip.....................A kind tongue ☐
☐ Swearing and profanity.........A reverent attitude ☐
☐ A quarrelsome spirit....A peace-loving disposition ☐
☐ Explosive behavior...................Self-control ☐
☐ Domineering attitudes.....Thoughtfulness of others ☐
☐ Boisterous rowdiness.............Ladylike reserve ☐
☐ False sophistication.....Sincerity and naturalness ☐
☐ Holding grudges..........Forgiving and forgetting ☐
☐ Over-display of self......Dignity and self-respect ☐
☐ Dishonorable actions.........Unblemished integrity ☐
☐ Becoming "cheap"..................Honor and virtue ☐
☐ Pessimism...............................Optimism ☐
☐ Conceit and vanity.........Modest self-confidence ☐
☐ Unchastity.........................Sexual purity ☐

NO, SHE'S NOT A BOY!
(She's just hidden her feminine qualities.)

_____ TOTAL   TOTAL _____

True Femininity

Is it curling the hair
    Or painting the face?
Pinning on bows,
    Pink ribbons and lace?
Flounces and frills,
    Bracelets and rings?
Polishing nails?
    Is it all of these things?

No, you can't pin it on
    Like a bow in the hair.
You can't put it on
    Like the garment you wear.
It's deeper than ornaments
    Gracing the skin.
For true femininity
    Comes from within!

It glows from a heart
    That is gentle and kind,
A soul that is chaste,
    An honest, pure mind.
Without inner goodness
    How futile the bows,
For "pinning on petals"
    Can n'er make a rose!

                --E.H.

Notes and Review

1. When choosing a hair style, I should consider the shape of my, _____ my facial _____ and my total body _____ .

2. My hair is an important outward characteristic of my _____ .

3. What was the symbolical meaning of a woman's long hair in Bible days?

4. In I Corinthians 11:15 we read that a woman's long hair is a _____ to her.

5. In Psalm 45:13 we read that the King's daughter is "all glorious _____ ."

6. What "inner" qualities give "feminine glory" to a daughter of the king?

Are My Hands Lovely?

LOVELY HANDS ARE CLEAN

Wash them often with lukewarm water and mild soap.
Bleach ink spots or stains with lemon or peroxide.
Scrub grimy knuckles. Attack imbedded dirt with brush.

LOVELY HANDS ARE SMOOTH

Pamper with lotion. Dry skin cracks and chaps.
Sand with pumice to remove callouses and rough spots.
Wear gloves to protect from harsh jobs and weather.

HAND LOTION   PUMICE   WORK GLOVES   MITTENS

LOVELY HANDS ARE MANICURED REGULARLY

1. Shape nails:
   Start at sides; file toward center.
   Avoid filing too deeply at corners of nails.
   Strive for a graceful oval contour.
   Avoid short stubs or long claws.

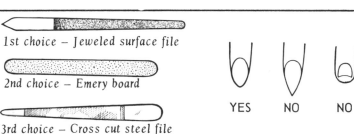

1st choice – Jeweled surface file

2nd choice – Emery board

3rd choice – Cross cut steel file

YES   NO   NO

2. Soak and clean:
   Soak fingers in warm, soapy water five minutes.
   Scrub knuckles and cuticles with brush.
   Scrub beneath nails.
   Finish cleaning nails with orange stick.

3. Push back cuticle:
   Soak cotton-tipped orange stick in cuticle remover.
   Thoroughly moisten each cuticle.
   Push back cuticle, lifting gently.
   Remove hangnails with nippers.

CUTICLE REMOVER

4. Apply polish:
   Do not use polish that has become thick.
   Apply polish with sweeping strokes as shown.
   Rub away a hairline of polish from tip of nail.
   Apply second coat when first is completely dry.

LOVELY HANDS ARE POISED

Nervous hand movements destroy charm. Avoid twisting, drumming, stroking, twiddling motions. To release tension, squeeze hands into tight fists, then release. Train hands to assume graceful postures.

SQUEEZE   RELEASE   NO   YES

'What is that in thine hand?'

(Exodus 4:2)

What do you clasp within your fingers from day to day? Some things should not be found in the hand of a lovely Christian girl, for they are poison to the mind, poison to the body, and poison to the soul!

● Hands Off!

"I will set no wicked thing before mine eyes" (Psalm 101:3).

"Whatsoever things are true,
whatsoever things are honest,
whatsoever things are just,
whatsoever things are pure,
whatsoever things are lovely,
whatsoever things are of good report;
if there be any virtue, and
if there be any praise,
think on these things" (Philippians 4:8).

"As he thinketh in his heart, so is he" (Proverbs 23:7).

● Hands Off!

"What? know ye not that your body is the temple of the Holy Ghost which is in you, which ye have of God, and ye are not your own? For ye are bought with a price: therefore glorify God in your body, and in your spirit, which are God's" (I Corinthians 6:19,20).

"If any man defile the temple of God, him shall God destroy; for the temple of God is holy, which temple ye are" (I Corinthians 3:17).

"Know ye not, that to whom ye yield yourselves servants to obey, his servants ye are" (Romans 6:16)?

"Of whom a man is overcome, of the same he is brought in bondage" (II Peter 2:19).

● Hands Off!

"Wine is a mocker, strong drink is raging: and whosoever is deceived thereby is not wise" (Proverbs 20:1).

"Who hath woe? who hath sorrow? who hath contentions? ...they that tarry long at the wine" (Proverbs 23:29,30).

"At the last it biteth like a serpent, and stingeth like an adder" (Proverbs 23:32).

"Now the works of the flesh are manifest, which are these: Adultery, fornication...drunkenness, revellings, and such like: of the which I tell you before, as I have also told you in time past, that they which do such things shall not inherit the kingdom of God" (Galatians 5:19-21).

Notes and Review

1. How does the grooming of my hands affect my self-confidence and social poise?

2. What nervous hand movements should I avoid?

3. How can hands be used as tools for God?

4. How can hands be used as tools for Satan?

5. The apostle Paul said, "Touch not the unclean thing" (II Corinthians 6:17).
   How can I apply this admonition to the use of my hands today?

How to Flatter my Figure

ARE YOU TALL?

DO WEAR...

Horizontal lines.
Full sleeves.
Wide yokes, collars or belts.
Contrasting tops and bottoms.

yes   *no*

AVOID...

Slim, one-piece dresses with
    vertical lines.
Very short, or very long
    sleeves.

ARE YOU PLUMP?

DO WEAR...

Up-and down lines.
Simple, tailored styles.
Neutral or dark colors.
Flared or A-line skirts.

yes   *no*

AVOID...

Horizontal contrasts.
Bold patterns.
Bulky styles with ruffles.
Full skirts and wide belts.

ARE YOU SHORT?

DO WEAR...

Up-and-down lines.
Simple styles, solid colors.
No belts or narrow belts.
Panels and princess lines.
Buttons from top to hem.

yes   *no*

AVOID...

Bulky tops.
Full skirts.
Large collars.
Horizontal contrasts.

ARE YOU THIN?

DO WEAR...

Full skirts.
Full sleeves.
Horizontal lines.
Plaids and prints.
Light, bright colors.

yes   *no*

AVOID...

Dark colors.
Vertical lines.
Tight-fitting clothes.

HEAVY AT THE HIP-LINE?

DO WEAR...

Flared or full skirts.
Skirts of darker colors
    than toppers.
Blouses with horizontal
    lines.

yes   *no*

AVOID...

Horizontal lines at hips.
Tight belts and tops.
Snug, clinging skirts.

FULL IN THE BOSOM?

DO WEAR...

Blouses of darker color
    than skirts.
Blouses with vertical
    lines.
Flared or A-line skirts.

yes   *no*

AVOID...

High, round necklines.
Wide belts and narrow skirts.
Horizontal bodice lines.

'Sizing up' my Figure

MY DOMINANT FIGURE FAULT IS:_____

_____

TECHNIQUES TO MINIMIZE IT: _____

_____

_____

_____

_____

_____

(Cut out pictures of fashion styles which you should follow to flatter your figure. Paste pictures below.)

STYLES I SHOULD WEAR TO FLATTER MY FIGURE...

What are my 'Spiritual Proportions?'

"That ye may stand perfect and complete in all the will of God" (Colossians 4:12).

"Till we all come . . . unto a perfect man, unto the measure of the stature of Christ" Ephesians 4:13.

AM I IN PERFECT FORM?

Head — Of moderate size, never "big-headed." "For I say... to every man...not to think of himself more highly than he ought to think" (Romans 12:3).

DO I HOLD TOO HIGH AN OPINION OF MYSELF? DO I ACT AS THOUGH I KNOW MORE THAN OTHERS?

☐ Seldom ☐ Occasionally ☐ Often

Shoulders — Broad enough to bear others' burdens. "Bear ye one another's burdens, and so fulfill the law of Christ" (Galatians 6:2).

WHEN DIFFICULTIES ARISE IN MY HOME, DO I CHEERFULLY DO MY PART TO LIGHTEN THE LOAD?

☐ Seldom ☐ Occasionally ☐ Always

Chest — Of normal dimension, not "puffed up." "Love vaunteth not itself, is not puffed up" (I Corinthians 13:4).

DO I PROUDLY FLAUNT NEW CLOTHES, GOOD GRADES, OR OTHER ACHIEVEMENTS BEFORE OTHERS?

☐ Seldom ☐ Occasionally ☐ Often

Back — Firm with a strong "back-bone." "Watch ye, stand fast in the faith...be strong" (I Corinthians 16:13).

DO I STAND FIRM AND SAY "NO" WHEN FRIENDS URGE ME TO DO WRONG?

☐ Seldom ☐ Occasionally ☐ Often

Knees — Limber, ready to kneel in submission. "Every knee shall bow to me...every one of us shall give account of himself to God" (Romans 14:11,12).

DO I SUBMIT MY CHOICE OF FRIENDS, MY AMUSEMENTS, MY AMBITIONS TO THE WILL OF GOD FOR MY LIFE?

☐ Seldom ☐ Occasionally ☐ Always

Feet — Sure-footed and confident. "He shall direct thy paths...thy foot shall not stumble" (Proverbs 3:6,23).

WHEN I HIT A SNAG OR ROCKY PATH IN MY TRYING TEEN YEARS, DO I TURN TO THE LORD FOR DIRECTION AND HELP?

☐ Seldom ☐ Occasionally ☐ Always

Notes and Review

1. What should be my attitude toward any figure faults or disproportions I may possess?

2. If I wear up-and-down lines, the eye senses _____ .

3. If I wear side-ways lines, the eye senses _____ .

4. If I wish to minimize a portion of my figure, I should choose a _____color.

5. If I wish to accentuate a portion of my figure, I should choose a _____color.

6. How can I give balance and pleasing proportion to my silhouette if my bustline is large? If my hip line is heavy?

7. Do all have perfect "spiritual proportions" (Romans 3:23)?

8. Who is our perfect standard by whom we measure ourselves (Ephesians 4:13)?

How Can I Look Well-Dressed?

I MUST LOOK UP-TO-DATE...

- Basic styles are long-lasting. Fads come and go.
- Pep up basics with current fads (belts, scarves, etc.)
- Sewing saves money. Adjust hems. Remodel styles.

I MUST BECOME COLOR-WISE...

My best colors are:

_____

(for wardrobe basics)

_____

(for accent colors)

I must wear:

- Intense colors in smaller doses.
- Only one vivid color at a time.
- Neutral colors for basic clothes.
- Bright colors for wardrobe accents.

I MUST MIX-AND-MATCH WITH SKILL...

yes   *no*   *yes*   *no*

- Combine "busy" tops with plain bottoms. Wear plain tops with "busy" skirts.
- Combine patterned tops with lowers of solid color. Wear solid color tops with patterned skirts.

I MUST DRESS WITH SIMPLICITY...

yes   *no*

I MUST DRESS APPROPRIATELY--THE RIGHT CLOTHES FOR THE OCCASION...

A special dress for a special occasion! Wear dressy shoes. Add a bit of jewelry and perfume.

DRESSY DATES

Look your best. Appear neither too party-ish nor too casual. Show respect for God's house by wearing clean, neat and respectable clothes.

CHURCH

Wear casual clothing-- jumpers and blouses, sweaters and skirts, simple dresses and everyday shoes.

EVERYDAY SCHOOL WEAR

The Christian Girl's Wardrobe

DOES
"BELONGING TO CHRIST"
MAKE A DIFFERENCE IN
THE WAY A GIRL
DRESSES ?

1. Yes! A Christian girl strives to please Christ in everything--including the way she dresses.

> "Whatsoever you do, do all to the glory of God" (I Corinthians 10:31).

2. She dresses with style and taste so that her appearance will bring honor to the One she represents.

> "Now then we are ambassadors for Christ" (II Corinthians 5:20).

3. She takes the Lord Jesus Christ shopping with her! As she stands before the mirror, she asks herself, "Would I want to meet Jesus looking like this?"

> "Not as pleasing men, but God" (I Thessalonians 2:4).

4. She avoids all that is gawdy and conspicuous, knowing this might focus so much attention on her outer appearance that it dims the beauty of Christ within.

> "Not I, but Christ liveth in me" (Galatians 2:20).

5. She tries not to look dull or drab, for she knows that unattractive dress is not befitting a daughter of the King.

> "The king's daughter is all glorious within: her clothing is of wrought gold" (Psalm 45:13).

6. She uses moderation in following fashion, seeking to be classed as neither "old-fashioned" nor "first in fashion."

> "Let your moderation be known unto all men" (Philippians 4:5).

> "Be not the first by whom the new is tried,
> Nor yet the last to lay the old aside."
> --Alexander Pope

7. She follows the styles of the crowd whenever possible, but refuses to conform when conformity requires a lowering of her standards.

> "And be not conformed to this world; but be ye transformed by the renewing of your mind" (Romans 12:2). "Hold fast that which is good" (I Thessalonians 5:21).

8. She does not use her clothing for vainglorious pomp and show.

"Let nothing be done through strife or vainglory; but in lowliness of mind" (Philippians 2:3).

"How proud we are! how fond to show
Our clothes, and call them rich and new!
When the poor sheep and silk-worm wore
That very clothing long before."
                                        --Isaac Watts

9. She does not overdress. She selects clothing which is appropriate to the occasion and beautiful in simplicity.

"In like manner also, that women adorn themselves in modest apparel...not with broided hair, or gold, or pearls, or costly array; but (which becometh women professing godliness) with good works" (I Timothy 2:9,10).

"Virtue is like a rich stone--best plain set." (Bacon)

10. She strives to look feminine. Being proud of the fact that God made her "a girl," she delights to dress like one!

"The woman shall not wear that which pertaineth unto a man" (Deuteronomy 22:5).

11. She refuses to "play up her sex," for she would not want to pin the label "cheap" or "common" on that which belongs to Christ.

"For ye are bought with a price: therefore glorify God in your body" (I Corinthians 6:20).

12. She avoids styles which are too bare or too revealing. She knows that she would be an accomplice in the sin, if her provocative attire aroused wrong thoughts in a fellow's mind.

"Whosoever looketh on a woman to lust after her hath committed adultery with her already in his heart" (Matthew 5:28).

"Modesty is the conscience of the body." (Balzac)

13. She realizes that modesty in dress brings not only God's approval, but also lasting admiration from the fellows, as they see in her the kind of girl they would someday want to marry.

"Who can find a virtuous woman? for her price is far above rubies. The heart of her husband doth safely trust in her" (Proverbs 31:10,11).

14. She refuses to become so fascinated by fashion books that she forsakes the Book of Books which guides her in the "fashioning" of her eternal soul.

"For the fashion of this world passeth away" (I Corinthians 7:31). "But the word of the Lord endureth for ever" (I Peter 1:25).

My 'Spiritual Clothing'
In God's Sight, How am I Dressed?

WHEN I STAND BEFORE GOD ONE DAY, WILL MY GARMENTS BE FIT FOR HEAVEN?

"I belong to a very respectable family. My grandfather was a minister. I live a clean, decent life. Don't drink, smoke, or swear like some girls! Never robbed a bank or killed anyone. I try to follow the Golden Rule. Of course, no one's perfect, but I'm just as good as the next one--if not a little bit better! I read to shut-ins, help my sick neighbors, run errands, and even do babysitting free! I'm no atheist...I believe in a Supreme Being...pray to Him if things get bad... and I go to Sunday School too! (Mom says it's the proper thing to do.) Sure I'll get to Heaven! If I can't make it, who can?"

"I'm a sinner... I could never become good enough for Heaven! God requires perfect holiness. I'm far from perfect! But I've asked Christ to be my Saviour. Now God sees me "in Christ," fit for Heaven! When Christ took my place on the cross, He took my sin-stained, filthy rags on Him--just as though every sin were His! He gave me His Spotless Robe of Righteousness-- just as though His Perfect Goodness were mine! What a wonderful exchange! I don't deserve it! It's simply a gift received by faith. Now I want to do good deeds because I love God. I want to please Him and serve Him!"

"BUT WE ARE ALL AS AN UNCLEAN THING, AND ALL OUR RIGHTEOUSNESSES ARE AS FILTHY RAGS" (ISAIAH 64:6).

"NOT OF WORKS, LEST ANY MAN SHOULD BOAST" (EPHESIANS 2:9).

"I WILL GREATLY REJOICE IN THE LORD. . . HE HATH COVERED ME WITH THE ROBE OF RIGHTEOUSNESS" (ISAIAH 61:10).

"FOR HE HATH MADE HIM TO BE SIN FOR US. . . THAT WE MIGHT BE MADE THE RIGHTEOUSNESS OF GOD IN HIM" (II CORINTHIANS 5:21).

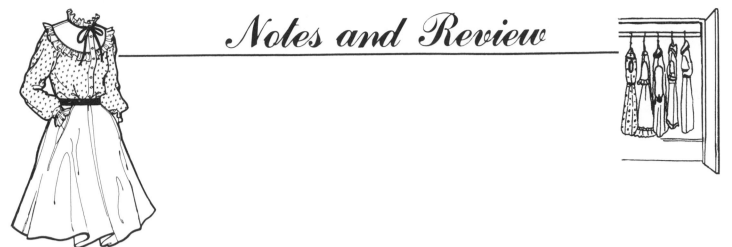

Notes and Review

1. *How do the clothes I wear affect others, myself, and my Christian witness?*

2. *What should I consider before I choose to imitate other girls in their dress?*

3. *How can a well-organized closet help my wardrobe planning?*

4. *What points should I check when trying on ready-to-wear garments?*

5. *What tailoring details are found on well-made garments?*

6. *What is the difference between looking "feminine" and merely looking "female"?*

7. *In what way can our manner of dress place a "stumbling block" in another's way? (See Romans 14:13 and I Corinthians 8:9).*

8. *What is the only garment that will make me fit to stand before God some day and how can I obtain it?*

Grooming Tips

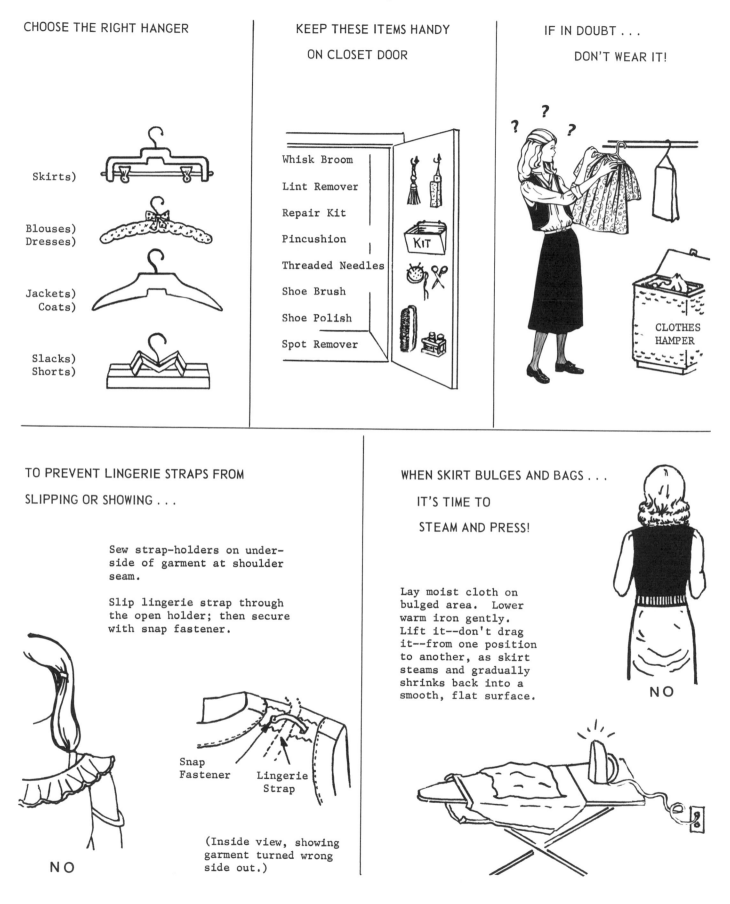

CHOOSE THE RIGHT HANGER

Skirts)

Blouses)
Dresses)

Jackets)
Coats)

Slacks)
Shorts)

KEEP THESE ITEMS HANDY

ON CLOSET DOOR

Whisk Broom

Lint Remover

Repair Kit

Pincushion

Threaded Needles

Shoe Brush

Shoe Polish

Spot Remover

KIT

IF IN DOUBT . . .

DON'T WEAR IT!

? ? ?
?

CLOTHES
HAMPER

TO PREVENT LINGERIE STRAPS FROM

SLIPPING OR SHOWING . . .

Sew strap-holders on under-
side of garment at shoulder
seam.

Slip lingerie strap through
the open holder; then secure
with snap fastener.

Snap
Fastener

Lingerie
Strap

NO

(Inside view, showing
garment turned wrong
side out.)

WHEN SKIRT BULGES AND BAGS . . .

IT'S TIME TO

STEAM AND PRESS!

Lay moist cloth on
bulged area. Lower
warm iron gently.
Lift it--don't drag
it--from one position
to another, as skirt
steams and gradually
shrinks back into a
smooth, flat surface.

NO

Am I Well-Groomed?

(Check items which are true of you. Add check-marks for total score.)

"MISS WELL-GROOMED"   "MISS CARELESS CATHY"

☐	My skin is fresh for I bathe each day.
☐	My hair is clean. Dirt is washed away.
☐	My nails are smooth--never chipped or long.
☐	My perfume's light--never "sickly strong."
☐	My clothes are neat--never pinned or tacked.
☐	My bag is clean--never jammed or packed.
☐	My makeup's light and with care applied.
☐	My shoes are polished, my laces tied.
☐	My skirt's well-pressed--not a bulge or bag.
☐	My slip hangs right--doesn't droop or sag.
☐	My blouse lies smooth, neatly tucked inside.
☐	My belt is flat--doesn't twist or "ride."
☐	I air my shoes, and I "talc" my feet.
☐	With sprays and creams, underarms stay sweet.
☐	I gargle mouth odor germs away.
☐	I brush my teeth to prevent decay.
☐	I shave my legs and my underarms.
☐	And sagging hose never spoil my charms.
☐	I rinse my undies afresh each night.
☐	I launder often to keep clothes bright.
☐	I air my clothes so they're odor-free.
☐	I hang them up very carefully.
☐	I sew loose buttons before they stray.
☐	I sew loose hems so they don't give way.
☐	I sew on each missing hook or snap.
☐	I sew split seams so they never gap.
☐	I anchor straps so they never slide.
☐	I tuck all facings and tags inside.

_____ MY TOTAL SCORE

RATING YOURSELF

Score of 23 to 28	Congratulations, "Miss Well-Groomed!" You are sure to please!
Score of 15 to 22	Improvements are needed! Smooth rough edges for a finer "polish."
Score of 0 to 14	Get organized now, "Miss Careless Cathy!" You are hiding your loveliness!

My Personal Grooming Chart

"HABITS ARE AT FIRST COBWEBS, THEN CABLES."
To form proper grooming habits, check items below for a 28-day period.

DAILY A. M.	1	2	3	4	5	6	7	8	9	10	11	12	13	14	15	16	17	18	19	20	21	22	23	24	25	26	27	28
Shower (optional)																												
Wash face																												
Wash underarms																												
Brush teeth																												
Mouthwash																												
Deodorant																												
Full Mirror Check																												
DAILY P. M.																												
Bath and cologne																												
Remove makeup																												
Wash face																												
Brush teeth																												
Brush hair																												
Air clothes																												
Wash undies																												
Plan-Ahead Check																												
WEEKLY (or as required)																												
Manicure																												
Pedicure																												
Shampoo																												
Shave legs, underarms																												
Clean and press clothes																												
Mend and repair clothes																												
Clean out purse																												
Tidy closet and drawers																												

DAILY A. M.
FULL LENGTH MIRROR CHECK-LIST

(Check front and back views.)

1. Skirt wrinkled?
2. Seams crooked?
3. Slip dangling?
4. Hose wrinkled?
5. Zipper unzipped?
6. Belt twisted?
7. Skirt off-center?
8. Straps showing?
9. Linings sagging?
10. Seams popped?
11. Rips or tears?
12. Spots or stains?
13. Loose buttons?
14. Dandruff speckles?
15. Lint or hairs?

DAILY P. M.
"PLAN-AHEAD" CHECK-LIST

1. Do I know what I will wear in the morning?
2. Have I chosen coordinating separates?
3. Have I laid out my accessories--jewelry, shoes, bag?
4. Have I laid out fresh lingerie and hose?
5. Is the slip the right style and length for my dress?

My 'Spiritual Grooming'

I look into God's Word... I look at myself... I look to God in prayer!

1.

2.

3.

"Let us cleanse ourselves from all filthiness of the flesh and spirit" (II Corinthians 7:1).

▶ DO I REMOVE THE ACCUMULATED SOIL EACH DAY WITH A CLEANSING "SPIRITUAL BATH"?

Make me clean today,
Cleanse my heart anew;
Wash my sins away,
Make me pure and true.

"You must stop letting any bad word pass your lips" (Ephesians 4:29, Williams).

▶ DO I SWEETEN MY BREATH REGULARLY WITH "GOD'S MOUTHWASH?"

Take my unclean lips!
With Thy touch erase
All that's coarse and foul.
Give me words of grace.

"Not having spot, or wrinkle... but that it should be holy and without blemish" (Ephesians 5:27).

▶ DO I APPLY "GOD'S SPOT-REMOVER" AND "SPIRITUAL BLEACH" TO MY BLEMISHES?

Remove each ugly spot!
Bleach each stubborn stain!
Make my garments white;
Let no smudge remain.

"Which look beautiful on the outside, but inside are full of... everything that is unclean" (Matthew 23:27, Williams)!

▶ DO I ALLOW THE PENETRATING ACTION OF "GOD'S DETERGENT" TO CLEANSE ME ALL THE WAY THROUGH?

Let me not deceive
In self-righteous pride,
With outer garments clean,
While hiding dirt inside.

"Forgetting those things which are behind, and reaching forth unto those things which are before" (Philippians 3:13).

▶ IS MY "SPIRITUAL CLOSET" CLOGGED WITH OLD "SKELETONS"?

May the closet of my soul
Be fresh and clean and free.
Though Satan should accuse,
I rest my case with Thee!

"He that covereth his sins shall not prosper" (Proverbs 28:13).

▶ DO I ATTEMPT TO COVER UP A LACK OF CLEANLINESS WITH THE PERFUME OF "PRETENDED PIETY"?

May the perfume of my prayer
Rise from a spirit true,
And never form a screen
To hide my sins from view.

"But we all, with open face beholding as in a glass the glory of the Lord, are changed into the same image from glory to glory" (II Corinthians 3:18).

▶ DO I REFLECT MORE AND MORE THE BEAUTY OF JESUS AS I GAZE INTO GOD'S MIRROR?

May I behold Thy Son
Each day within Thy Word.
May I reflect His face
With radiance unblurred!

Notes and Review

1. Why is "cleanliness first" the basic rule in all good grooming?

2. What items should my handbag contain?

3. What steps should I take before hanging a garment in my closet?

4. When I neglect my grooming, what am I saying to the world?

5. If the world accepts my self-appraisal, what naturally follows?

6. Why should a Christian girl be especially careful not to place a low "price tag" on herself? (See I Peter 1:18, 19).

7. What is the miracle cleansing agent that removes spiritual stains (I John 1:7) and how is it applied?

Eating Gracefully

Do you resemble any of these three girls?

THE "HOSTESS HARASSER"

This girl gives her hostess a bad time. She's not only insensitive to her feelings but also fails to show her customary courtesy and respect.

1. She carelessly arrives late, causing her hostess to keep dinner waiting.

2. She plops down without waiting for her hostess to be seated or to tell her where to sit.

3. She surveys the table and then asks for some non-essential item not on the table.

4. She rests her shoes on the legs of the costly chairs.

5. She calls loud attention to the hair in her salad or the stain on her drinking glass.

6. She talks endlessly, lagging behind the others, and forcing the hostess to delay serving the next course.

7. She helps herself to huge helpings of choice, precious food items, then leaves a large portion uneaten.

THE "THOUGHTLESS DINNER GUEST"

This girl is inconsiderate of the other guests. Thinking only of her own needs, she fails to consider the needs and feelings of those around her.

1. She hastily sits down before the man or boy at her left has time to help her into her seat thus denying him the privilege of acting gentlemanly.

2. She stretches her legs out, taking more than her share of space beneath the table.

3. She tries to "long arm" it over the plates of others to get items she wants.

4. She ponders over each serving dish, making others wait while she searches for the piece she prefers. After helping herself, she sets the dish down, forgetting to pass it on.

5. She puts her soiled utensils in the common serving dishes. She dips her wet teaspoon in the sugar bowl.

6. She fingers several cookies or rolls before taking one.

7. She jabs her elbows into those beside her when she cuts her meat.

8. She empties out the serving dish without considering that others might want "seconds" too!

"MISS DISPLEASING"

Because this girl's table manners (both "audio and visual") are unpleasant to be around, she spoils the appetites of all!

1. She bolts her food as though starved! She encircles her plate with her arm, and (like an animal) crouches over it, lowering her head to her food rather than lifting her food to her mouth.

2. She chews noisily, slurps liquids loudly and smacks her lips. She burps without attempting to stifle it.

3. Because she talks with food in her mouth and chews with her mouth open, others must view the chewed-up food inside her mouth.

4. She uses her fingers as "food pushers" and then extends her tongue and licks her fingers clean. She digs at food lodged between her teeth.

5. She drinks with one continuous gulp, then exhales loudly across the table. She drinks with greasy, sticky lips, thus leaving a smear around the rim of her drinking glass.

6. She pulls out a soiled handkerchief and blows her nose loud and long across the table.

7. She discusses subjects revolting to the senses.

Do you know what the girl with good training does?

How well can you answer these questions? Check your selections. (There may be more than one right answer to a question.) When correcting your answers, mark each right answer with a "C" so that you will be able to use the answers as a guide to what the well mannered girl should do.

1. **When does the well-mannered girl start eating?**

   At a small dinner party of 6 or fewer guests:

   (a) ☐ Whenever she feels like it, depending on how hungry she is.

   (b) ☐ After everyone else has been served and the hostess has begun.

   (c) ☐ As soon as she is served her food.

   At a large dinner party:

   (a) ☐ After everyone has been served and the hostess has begun.

   (b) ☐ After 4 or 5 have been served, or the hostess says, "Please go ahead, so the food won't get cold!"

2. **Does she ever place her elbows on the table?**

   (a) ☐ Yes, when she is tired.

   (b) ☐ No, never!

   (c) ☐ Never while she is eating, but perhaps while resting between courses or conversing at the end of the meal.

3. **Where does she leave her napkin throughout the meal?**

   (a) ☐ On her lap.

   (b) ☐ Tucked under her chin.

   (c) ☐ Tied around her neck.

   (d) ☐ On the table.

4. **What does she do with her napkin when she leaves the table?**

   (a) ☐ She refolds it the same way she found it.

   (b) ☐ She wads it up and puts it on her chair.

   (c) ☐ She lays it in loose folds beside her plate.

5. **How does she pass a pitcher?**

   (a) ☐ She hands it to the next person with the handle turned toward that person.

   (b) ☐ She sets it on the table in front of the next person.

6. **What does she do if the hostess serves food she doesn't like?**

   (a) ☐ She advises her that she won't eat any of that particular food, because she can't stand it!

   (b) ☐ She keeps quiet about it and takes a small portion anyway.

   (c) ☐ She takes some, but hides it in her napkin.

7. **How does she serve herself gravy from the gravy boat?**

   (a) ☐ She simply pours it out.

   (b) ☐ She spoons it out with her own spoon.

   (c) ☐ She dips gravy with the gravy ladle.

8. **When butter or jelly is passed, where does she place it?**

   (a) ☐ She puts it on her plate, then transfers it to her bread or roll.

   (b) ☐ She places it directly onto her bread or roll.

9. **When "finger foods" such as olives, cookies, or sandwiches are passed around the table, what does she do with them?**

   (a) ☐ She places them on her plate, then transfers them to her mouth.

   (b) ☐ She puts them directly into her mouth.

   (c) ☐ She puts them on the table beside her plate to eat later.

10. **How does she know which silver to use?**

    (a) ☐ As a general rule, she starts with the silver closest to her plate, then works toward the outside as the meal progresses.

    (b) ☐ She starts at the outside and works in toward her plate as the meal progresses.

    (c) ☐ When in doubt, she follows the lead of her hostess.

11. **What does she do with her knife and fork after using them?**

    (a) ☐ She lays them down on the tablecloth, flat.

    (b) ☐ She props the utensils against her plate with the handles resting on the table.

    (c) ☐ She lays them flat across the side of her plate.

    (d) ☐ She returns them to the same position they came from, beside her plate.

12. **What does she do with her silver when passing her plate for "seconds"?**

    (a) ☐ She holds them upright in her hand.

    (b) ☐ She lays her knife and fork side by side across her plate.

13. **How much meat does she cut at one time?**

    (a) ☐ She cuts most of the meat on her plate before she starts to eat it.

    (b) ☐ She cuts one bite at a time as she eats it.

14. What implements could she use on the following items?	(1) Dinner knife	(2) Butter spread-er	(3) Salad or dessert fork	(4) Dinner fork	(5) Soup spoon	(6) Tea-spoon	(7) Oyster fork	Fin-gers	Can you identify these? Place implement number in space provided below:
Fresh grapes, cherries, plums									
Pickles, radishes, olives									
French-fried potatoes									
Corn on the cob									
Pudding, custard, ice cream									
Fried chicken									
Sandwiches									
Moist cake									
Celery or carrot sticks									
Mashed potatoes and gravy									
Baked potato									
Nuts and mints									
Cantaloupe section									
Watermelon section									
Seafood cocktail									
Pie with ice cream									
To butter corn on the cob:									
To butter baked potato:									
To butter bread or roll:									

15. How does she butter her bread?

(a) ☐ She breaks off and butters a portion at a time.

(b) ☐ She butters the entire slice at one time.

(c) ☐ She holds bread in the palm of her hand when buttering it.

(d) ☐ She holds it flat on the table.

(e) ☐ She holds it on her plate (or slightly above).

16. How does she eat her soup?

(a) ☐ She dips her soup spoon toward her body.

(b) ☐ She dips her soup spoon away from her body.

(c) ☐ She sips from the side of the spoon.

(d) ☐ She sips from the end of the spoon.

(e) ☐ She crumples large crackers into her soup.

(f) ☐ She holds large crackers in her hand, but puts small oyster crackers in her soup, a few at a time.

17. How does she remove seeds, pits, gristle from her mouth?

(a) ☐ She takes unchewable food items out of her mouth in the same way they went in--with her fingers, fork, or spoon.

(b) ☐ She puts her napkin over her mouth, so no one will see her remove them.

(c) ☐ She spits them into her plate in full view.

(d) ☐ She drops them into her napkin, then covers it over.

18. How does she handle problems or accidents at the table?

(a) ☐ In a prolonged siege of coughing or choking, she leaves the table.

(b) ☐ She apologizes and sticks it out.

(c) ☐ If she drops silver, she picks it up and resumes using it, saying nothing.

(d) ☐ She leaves it on the floor until the end of the meal, and asks for a replacement if needed.

(e) ☐ If she spills food and it's causing no harm, she goes on as though nothing had happened.

(f) ☐ She calls attention to it and makes a big fuss apologizing.

(g) ☐ If she splatters food on someone else, she apologizes and immediately offers her napkin.

(h) ☐ She says, "Oops!" and laughs it off as a joke.

19. If the hostess lingers at the table following the meal, what does she do?

(a) ☐ She tells her she's tired of sitting and asks to be excused.

(b) ☐ She stays at the table until the hostess rises and says, "Shall we go into the living room?"

(c) ☐ If she has a pressing problem, she simply asks to be excused without making explanation.

HOW TO PERMIT A GENTLEMAN TO SEAT YOU AT THE TABLE

WHAT TO DO WITH YOUR KNIFE AND FORK AFTER USING THEM

He will pull chair away from table far enough to allow you to _____ .

He will slide chair forward as you _____ _____ . Keep your back _____ .

He will adjust chair closer to the table if you _____ again slightly.

NO

NO

YES
This position is correct when resting during the meal, when passing plate for "seconds," or when finished eating.

How to Make Introductions

1. Whom do I introduce to whom?

Introduce a younger person to an older person,
a boy to a girl,
a man to a woman,*
a young person to your parents.
Introduce your mother or father to your friend's mother or father,
your mother or father to your school principal or teacher.

* A girl enters this category around 18.

2. Are first names enough in an introduction?

Always include last names. One exception: When introducing members of your family whose last names are the same as yours. If your parents' name differs from yours, give the last name. For example: "This is my mother, Mrs. Carter."

3. What do I do when I am introduced?

Stand up.
Look at the person.
Say, "How do you do" or simply, "Hello."

Shake hands if the other person extends the hand. (A man waits for a woman or girl to offer her hand first.)

4. Is it proper to introduce myself?

Yes. This often eases an awkward situation. If possible, give some personal identification, such as, "I'm Betty Roberts, Tom's sister."

5. How do I introduce a newcomer to a group?

Announce the name of the newcomer to the group, then name the individual members of the group one by one: "This is Jane Grey, girls...and this is Sue Dunn, Linda Hood, Pam Wells, Jean Miller, etc."

6. If someone stops by my table in a restaurant, should I introduce him to the others eating with me?

Yes, if the person lingers. Otherwise, don't detain him. Let him go on his way with only a brief greeting.

Following the above instructions, fill in the blanks below with appropriate introductions.

Notes and Review

1. *What is the "golden rule" of all etiquette?*

2. *Why should correct table manners be practiced at home as well as in company?*

3. *Why should a Christian be especially concerned about developing lovely, courteous manners?*

4. *How do polite manners show honor and respect to others?   See Romans 12:10.*

5. *In I Peter 3:8, we read, "Love as brethren, be pitiful, be ————————————."*

CREATE IN ME THY BEAUTY NOW

Words by
Emily Hunter

Music by
Joyce Burch

Other Good Harvest House Reading

CHRISTIAN CHARM COURSE, Teacher Manual
by *Emily Hunter*

Step-by-step directions for class instruction, charm demonstrations, activities, and correlated spiritual emphasis.

MAN IN DEMAND
by *Wayne and Emily Hunter*

This personal development program shows that true manliness requires development of moral and spiritual strengths as well as physical and social. The training workbook is fully illustrated with teaching cartoons, quizzes, charts, self-inventories, diagrams, and spiritual challenges to capture the interest of teenage boys.

MAN IN DEMAND, Teacher Manual
by *Wayne and Emily Hunter*

Gives word-for word class instruction, together with directions for special demonstrations, activities, object lessons, and skits.

THE BONDAGE BREAKER YOUTH EDITION
by *Neil T. Anderson and Dave Park*

Here's help for youth who face peer pressure, sexual temptation, insecurity, and fear. Shows teens how to experience true freedom in Christ as they break free of even the most dangerous habits and sins.

HOW CAN I BE SURE?
by *Bob Phillips*

A pre-marriage inventory especially for counselors and pastors to use with young people in pre-marriage counseling or for young couples who are contemplating marriage. Now couples can explore one another's thoughts and feelings and find areas of agreement and a basis for resolving disagreements.

PURITY UNDER PRESSURE
by *Neil Anderson* and *Dave Park*

In a reassuring style, popular spiritual conflicts counselor Neil Anderson and Freedom in Christ youth director Dave Park help teens grasp the spiritual truths behind the pressures and temptations they face. They provide powerful tools and step-by-step instructions on breaking free from sin patterns and building godly relationships. Ideally suited for youth groups or individual study.